Weather
Sun

by Brienna Rossiter

FOCUS READERS
SCOUT

www.focusreaders.com

Copyright © 2020 by Focus Readers, Lake Elmo, MN 55042. All rights reserved. No part of this book may be reproduced or utilized in any form or by any means without written permission from the publisher.

Focus Readers is distributed by North Star Editions:
sales@northstareditions.com | 888-417-0195

Produced for Focus Readers by Red Line Editorial.

Photographs ©: AlinaMD/Shutterstock Images, cover, 13; Valeriy Boyarskiy/Shutterstock Images, 4; Pavel_Klimenko/Shutterstock Images, 7 (top), 16 (top right); Kotenko Oleksandr/Shutterstock Images, 7 (bottom), 16 (top left); Aphelleon/Shutterstock Images, 9, 16 (bottom left); Alexey Repka/Shutterstock Images, 11; Susan Schmitz/Shutterstock Images, 15; ESA/Hubble/NASA Goddard/Goddard Space Flight Center/NASA, 16 (bottom right)

Library of Congress Cataloging-in-Publication Data
Names: Rossiter, Brienna, author.
Title: Sun / by Brienna Rossiter.
Description: Lake Elmo, MN : Focus Readers, [2020] | Series: Weather | Audience: K to grade 3. | Includes index.
Identifiers: LCCN 2018060594 (print) | LCCN 2019000533 (ebook) | ISBN 9781644930090 (PDF) | ISBN 9781641859301 (ebook) | ISBN 9781641857925 (hardcover) | ISBN 9781641858618 (pbk.).
Subjects: LCSH: Sunshine--Juvenile literature. | Day--Juvenile literature. | Sun--Juvenile literature.
Classification: LCC QC911.2 (ebook) | LCC QC911.2 .R67 2020 (print) | DDC 523.7--dc23
LC record available at https://lccn.loc.gov/2018060594

Printed in the United States of America
Mankato, MN
May, 2019

About the Author

Brienna Rossiter is a writer and editor who lives in Minnesota. She loves learning random facts by reading books, going to museums, and traveling to new places.

Glossary

clouds

rays

Earth

star

Index

L
light, 5, 8

M
morning, 12

N
night, 14

S
star, 8

Table of Contents

What Is Sun? 5

How Sun Shines 8

Times of Day 12

Glossary 16

Index 16

What Is Sun?

Sun is light.

Sun is bright.

Sun is warm.

Sun shines in **rays**.

Clouds block rays.

Clouds make skies dark.

How Sun Shines

The sun is a **star**.

It gives off light.

The light shines on **Earth**.

Earth turns.

The sun shines on one side.

The other side is dark.

Times of Day

Earth turns toward the sun.

We see a sunrise.

It is morning.

Earth turns away from the sun.

We see a sunset.

Night is coming.